COUNTY DURHAM IN PHOTOGRAPHS

NATHAN ATKINSON

AMBERLEY

First published 2018

Amberley Publishing
The Hill, Stroud
Gloucestershire, GL5 4EP

www.amberley-books.com

ISBN 978 1 4456 8145 0 (print)
ISBN 978 1 4456 8146 7 (ebook)

British Library Cataloguing in Publication Data.
A catalogue record for this book is available from the British Library.

Origination by Amberley Publishing.
Printed in the UK.

INTRODUCTION

County Durham has had numerous boundary changes in the recent past. I was born in Stockton-on-Tees, which at that time was part of the county of Cleveland. The county of Cleveland was abolished in 1996, separating into several unitary authorities. This caused a bit of an issue when I was asked to create this book: which boundary should I use? I settled on the ceremonial boundary of County Durham so that the locations of Stockton, Darlington and Hartlepool were included.

Although I was brought up in the area, the majority of my landscape work took place in Cumbria or North Yorkshire. This wasn't ever a conscious decision and maybe was down to taking the local area for granted. In any case, I was keen to show our industrial heritage as well as the gorgeous landscapes the county provides. I have tried to show very recognisable places as well as the ones that are more locally known so that the book appeals to all.

While compiling this book I have met many people and been to many new places, as well as old haunts. A particular visit I was very excited about was to the Darlington Locomotive Works. Many will be aware that Darlington has a long historic connection with railways and some of the buildings remain that are part of our steam heritage. The A1 Steam Locomotive Trust occupy part of this historic building and constructed the world-renowned *Tornado* locomotive here. They are currently undertaking another huge project, namely the Gresley Class P2, No. 2007, *Prince of Wales*. It's not every day that you can photograph a steam locomotive being built, particularly one built locally.

As many photographers will tell you, the same place can look very different depending on the time of day, time of year and the weather conditions. Some outings just didn't work: the light was wrong or the weather forecast was unfavourable. My advice to anyone starting out in the field of photography is not to be disheartened if you spend a day out but the resultant photographs are lacking. It happens to the professionals too.

Were 126 pictures enough to show off the region? At the start of this project I would have said 'yes', but ask me now and the answer is firmly 'no'. There are some well-known places and attractions I haven't been able to include. This is both down to running out of time and some places/attractions having strict rules over commercial photography.

I hope you enjoy the book. Now to start work on my next Amberley adventure.

MORE INFORMATION

More information on some of the locations I have photographed can be accessed via the following links:
This is Durham: www.thisisdurham.com
No. 2007 *Prince of Wales*: www.p2steam.com
(or email enquiries@p2steam.com)
Killhope Lead Mining Museum: www.killhope.org.uk
Brancepeth Castle: www.brancepethcastle.org.uk
Bowes Museum: www.thebowesmuseum.org.uk
Preston Park Museum: www.prestonparkmuseum.co.uk
Hardwick Park: www.durham.gov.uk/hardwickpark

ABOUT THE PHOTOGRAPHER

Nathan Atkinson is a freelance photographer based in County Durham. Nathan started becoming interested in photography twenty years ago, initially focusing on landscapes in the north of England through his interest in the outdoors. In the past few years he has expanded his photography into other fields such as street and portrait.

Nathan currently has photographs adorning the cover of two Ordnance Survey maps: *Middlesbrough and Hartlepool, Stockton-on-Tees and Redcar* (OS Explorer Paper Map, 306) and *Middlesbrough, Darlington & Hartlepool* (OS Landranger Map, 93). He has also had photographs featured in the Children in Need BBC Look North (North East and Cumbria) calendar.

Website: www.miura-photography.co.uk
Facebook: @miuraphotography
Twitter: @Nathan_Lakes
Email: nathan@miura-photography.co.uk

ACKNOWLEDGEMENTS

I would like to dedicate this book to my kids, Blake and Ursula, for teaching me that when everything gets on top of you, either playing computer games or singing will get you out of it.

I would also like to thank a number of people who have helped me over the years with my photography and without whom this book would never exist. First of all, the love of my life, Sorcha. Putting up with my early starts, late starts and quick vanishing acts to get that specific shot is not an easy thing to do. Always supportive and never an eyelid batted when I'm in the middle of nowhere at three in the morning. Also, my Mum and Peter, Gordon and Sue for the support you have given me in my endeavours to improve my photography. Long may the Christmas calendars continue. My late friend Leigh Lee, the memories and the laughs we had even though nearly every outing resulted in bad weather!

There are two people who have been key to developing my skills. Firstly, David Bond, whom all of my basic knowledge and understanding came from. His explanations on how things worked were brilliant and his critical eye was very much appreciated. Secondly, Paul Moore, who has really pushed me in the past few years and helped me fine-tune my skills, even pushing me out of my comfort zone at times. Again, his critical eye is always welcome.

I also need to thank everyone at the A1 Steam Locomotive Trust, particularly Gemma Braithwaite and Daniela Filová for organising my visit to see the work being done on the *Prince of Wales* locomotive. The visit made me even more proud of my region.

After many attempts, I finally managed to photograph Killhope Lead Mining Museum. Apologies to Paul Leonard for the constant barrage of emails attempting to get there when the weather was right.

Thanks to Alison Hobbs at Brancepeth Castle for allowing me to use the location for a couple of shots – a stunning building and grounds.

Further acknowledgements to: Paul Mooney from *BBC Look North* (North East and Cumbria), Peter Simpson for a long list of places to visit and motivational support, Middleton-in-Teesdale Fish and Chip Shop for giving me sustenance in the middle of winter, Sheila Dixon from Bowes Museum, Ruby Wills at Stockton Borough Council, Lindsay Archer at Durham County Council, James Stamp from Formatt Hitech Filters and of course, Nick Grant and Jenny Stephens at Amberley Publishing.

SPRING

Sunny daffodil, South Park

Sunset over the Tees

Sunset, Archdeacon Newton

South Park, Darlington

Oil seed field, near Darlington

Teesdale stars

Crocuses in flower, Darlington

Green fields, near Wynyard

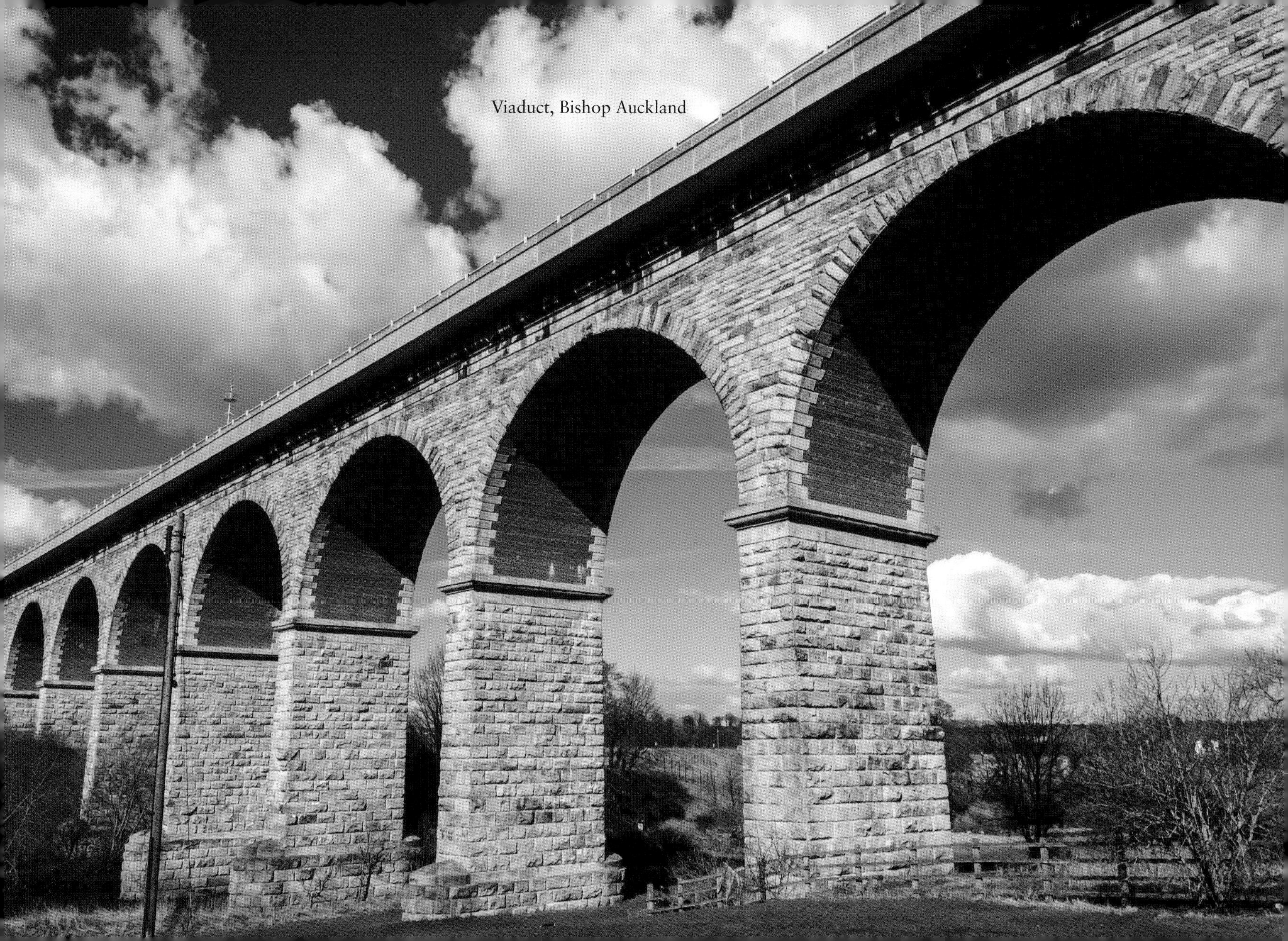

Viaduct, Bishop Auckland

Bandstand, Stockton

Ropner Park, Stockton

Quarry, near Bishopley

Tees Barrage

Sunrise at the turbines, North Gare

Turbines at sea, North Gare

Bluebells,
Durham

Evening sun at Cow Green

Infinity Bridge, Stockton-on-Tees

Sunrise over Hury

Whitfield Brow

Teesmouth

Spring gentians, near Cow Green

St Brandon's Church, Brancepeth

MATTERSON
S.W.L.
20 TONNES
SWL 40 TONNES

Above and opposite: *Prince of Wales* under construction

Whorlton Falls

SUMMER

Coatham Mundeville

Croxdale Viaduct

Finchale Priory

Low Force, Teesdale

Gibson's Cave

Wildflower meadow, near Haughton

Brancepeth Castle

Ferryhill Carrs

Wolf Cleugh, Weardale

Sunderland Bridge

Killhope Lead Mining Museum

Bow Lee Beck

The last rays of sun

Temple at sunset, Hardwick Park

Temple at sunset, Hardwick Park

Winged Victory, Hartlepool Headland

AUTUMN

Tommy at sunrise, Seaham

Sunrise, Seaham Harbour

Steetley Pier, Hartlepool

Steetley Pier, Hartlepool

Castle at night, Durham

Durham Cathedral during Lumiere

Ruined mine buildings, Weardale

Entering County Durham, Weardale

Hamsterley waterfall

Transporter Bridge, Port Clarence

Egglestone Abbey silhouette

Sunrise at Seal Sands

Sunrise, Seaham Harbour

Morning wave, Seaton Carew

Trees in the sun, Darlington

Skerne Bridge, Darlington

Autumn leaves and reflections, Hamsterley

Barnard Castle reflections at night

Hartlepool Marina

Hartlepool Headland

Grove Rake headgear

Durham Coast

Lunton Hill, Hamsterley

Lunton Hill, Hamsterley

South Park, Darlington

Misty sunset, Darlington

Seal Sands industry

Light trails, Greatham

Weardale

Tommy, Seaham

Crimdon Dene, Hartlepool

Rookhope Arch

Fir cones, Hamsterley Forest

Gnarled tree, Lunton Hill

WINTER

Robin in the snow, Pow Hill

Snow-covered Teesdale

River Tees, near High Force

High Force, Teesdale

Antiques shop, Middleton-in-Teesdale

Winter snowfall, Middleton-in-Teesdale

Up through the frosty trees, Darlington

Sunrise, Blackhall Rocks

Egglestone Abbey in the frost

Green Lane Winter, Darlington

Misty night, Stockton-on-Tees

Infinity Bridge, Stockton-on-Tees

River Tees, near Egglestone Abbey

Cotherstone stone cottages

Bowes Museum, Barnard Castle

Tree skyline, near Staindrop

Heavy snowfall, Middleton-in-Teesdale

Bleabeck Force, Teesdale

Raby Castle

Raby Castle in the snow

Sunset near Royal Oak

Blackhall Rock Caves

Moss-covered wall, near Bollihope

Bollihope Burn

Snowy rooftops, Middleton-in-Teesdale

Wintering sheep, near Middleton-in-Teesdale

Newport Bridge, Haverton Hill

Newport Bridge, Haverton Hill

Cotherstone

Red squirrel, Derwent Reservoir

Christmas at Preston Park Museum

Christmas at Preston Park Museum

Overlooking Teesdale

Romaldkirk Cottage

Kirkcarrion

Sunrise, Durham Coast

Horden mining sculpture

Unnamed reservoir, near Juniper Banks

Crepuscular rays over the Tees

Kirkcarrion

Seascape, Durham Coast

Darlington fog at Christmas

Snow near Selset

St Cuthbert's Church, Darlington

Market Cross, Barnard Castle

Old mine workings, near Bridget Hill

Selset Reservoir